# THE BATTLE OF THE ALAMO
## IGNITES INDEPENDENCE

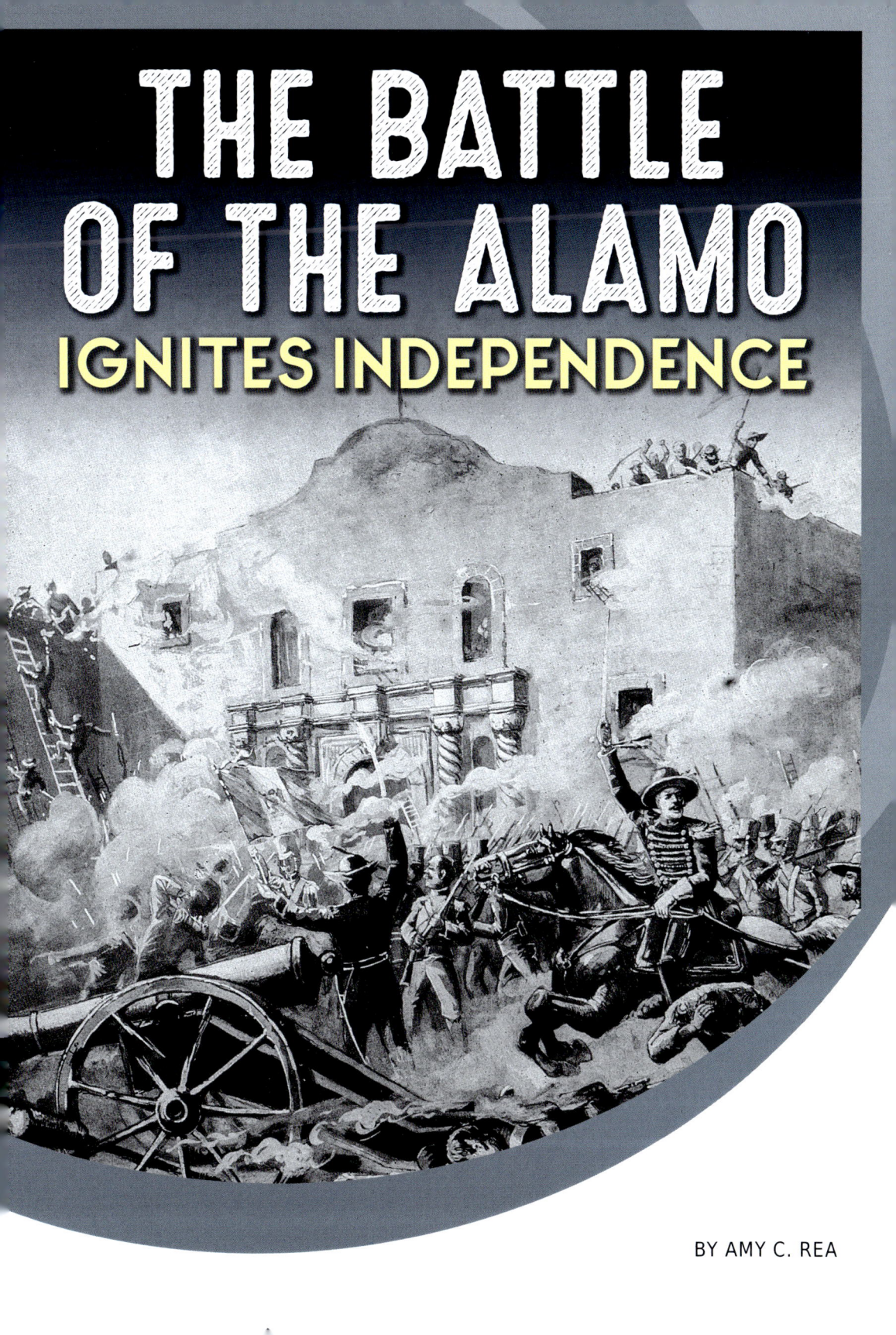

BY AMY C. REA

Published by The Child's World®
1980 Lookout Drive • Mankato, MN 56003-1705
800-599-READ • www.childsworld.com

Photographs ©: Kean Collection/Staff/Archive Photos/Getty Images, cover; Everett Historical/Shutterstock Images, 6, 10, 26; iStockphoto, 8, 20, 22, 24; Library of Congress, 11; Carol M. Highsmith/The Lyda Hill Texas Collection of Photographs/Carol M. Highsmith's America Project/Library of Congress, 13; North Wind Picture Archives, 14; Omikron/Science Source, 16; 3LH/SuperStock, 17; Augustine Chang/iStockphoto, 19; Niday Picture Library/Alamy, 23, 27; Everett Collection Historical/Alamy, 28

Copyright © 2019 by The Child's World®
All rights reserved. No part of this book may be reproduced or utilized in any form or by any means without written permission from the publisher.

ISBN 9781503825192
LCCN 2017959670

Printed in the United States of America
PA02376

## ABOUT THE AUTHOR

Amy C. Rea grew up in northern Minnesota and now lives in a Minneapolis suburb with her husband, two sons, and dog. She writes frequently about traveling around Minnesota.

# TABLE OF CONTENTS

**FAST FACTS AND TIMELINE** ..... 4

## Chapter 1
BEGINNING OF THE BATTLE ... 6

## Chapter 2
THE BATTLE OF THE ALAMO .. 14

## Chapter 3
THE BATTLE ENDS ............. 20

## Chapter 4
AFTER THE ALAMO ............ 24

Think About It  29
Glossary  30
Source Notes  31
To Learn More  32
Index  32

# FAST FACTS

## Who owned Texas in the mid-1830s?

- In 1835, the land now known as Texas belonged to Mexico. Mexico's president was Antonio López de Santa Anna.

## Who lived in Texas?

- The Mexican government allowed U.S. settlers to settle in the northern part of Mexico in the early 1800s. But as more U.S. citizens arrived there, tensions between U.S. citizens and Mexican citizens began to rise.
- Soon there were more U.S. citizens in Texas than there were people from Mexico. Their ties to the United States were strong.

## Why was there conflict between Texas and Mexico?

- As the U.S. population in Texas grew, many people wanted to break away from Mexico's rule.
- The U.S. government wanted to acquire Texas in order to expand the United States. The Mexican government was opposed to that idea.

# TIMELINE

December 5–9, 1835: The Texans and Mexicans battle for the control of the Alamo and San Antonio, which are in present-day Texas. The Texans win.

February 23, 1836: Santa Anna arrives at San Antonio with a much larger army than the Texans have. They surround the Alamo and begin a 13-day **siege**.

March 6, 1836: The Mexicans attack and take over the Alamo, killing all the Texan fighting men there.

April 21, 1836: The Texans, led by General Sam Houston, launch a surprise attack against Santa Anna's forces along the San Jacinto River. Despite having half as many soldiers as the Mexicans, the Texans win.

## Chapter 1

# BEGINNING OF THE BATTLE

On December 4, 1835, Ben Milam rode into the Texans' army camp near present-day San Antonio. His horse trotted past rows of dusty tents. Soldiers milled about. The sound of laughter reached Milam's ears. Some soldiers waved to him. He stayed on his horse until he reached General Edward Burleson's tent.

◀ Sam Houston served in the House of Representatives before becoming the governor of Tennessee. He moved to Texas in 1832.

The Texan soldiers there were engaging in the Siege of Bexar. Milam was a member of the army. He wanted to fight for Texas's independence. The Texas Revolution had begun in October 1835. In 1836, Texas would declare independence from Mexico and form the **Republic** of Texas.

The Texans had been planning to attack the Mexican forces at San Antonio, but Burleson had called them off. Milam believed this was the wrong decision. He felt that if the Texans did not attack, Texas's fight for independence was endangered. As he reached Burleson's tent, he jumped off his horse and hurried into the tent with hopes of changing Burleson's mind. The general crossed his arms and listened to Milam's complaints. He told Milam that the order to retreat had come from General Sam Houston. But Burleson said if Milam could get enough volunteers, he could go ahead with the attack on San Antonio.

Milam left the tent, waving his hat in the air. Excitedly, he shouted into the winter wind, "Who will follow old Ben Milam to San Antonio?"[1] Approximately 300 men volunteered. There was little sleep for them that cold, dark night as they prepared for battle. The soldiers grew excited but anxious. They knew what they were about to do was very dangerous.

# BATTLES IN THE TEXAS REVOLUTION

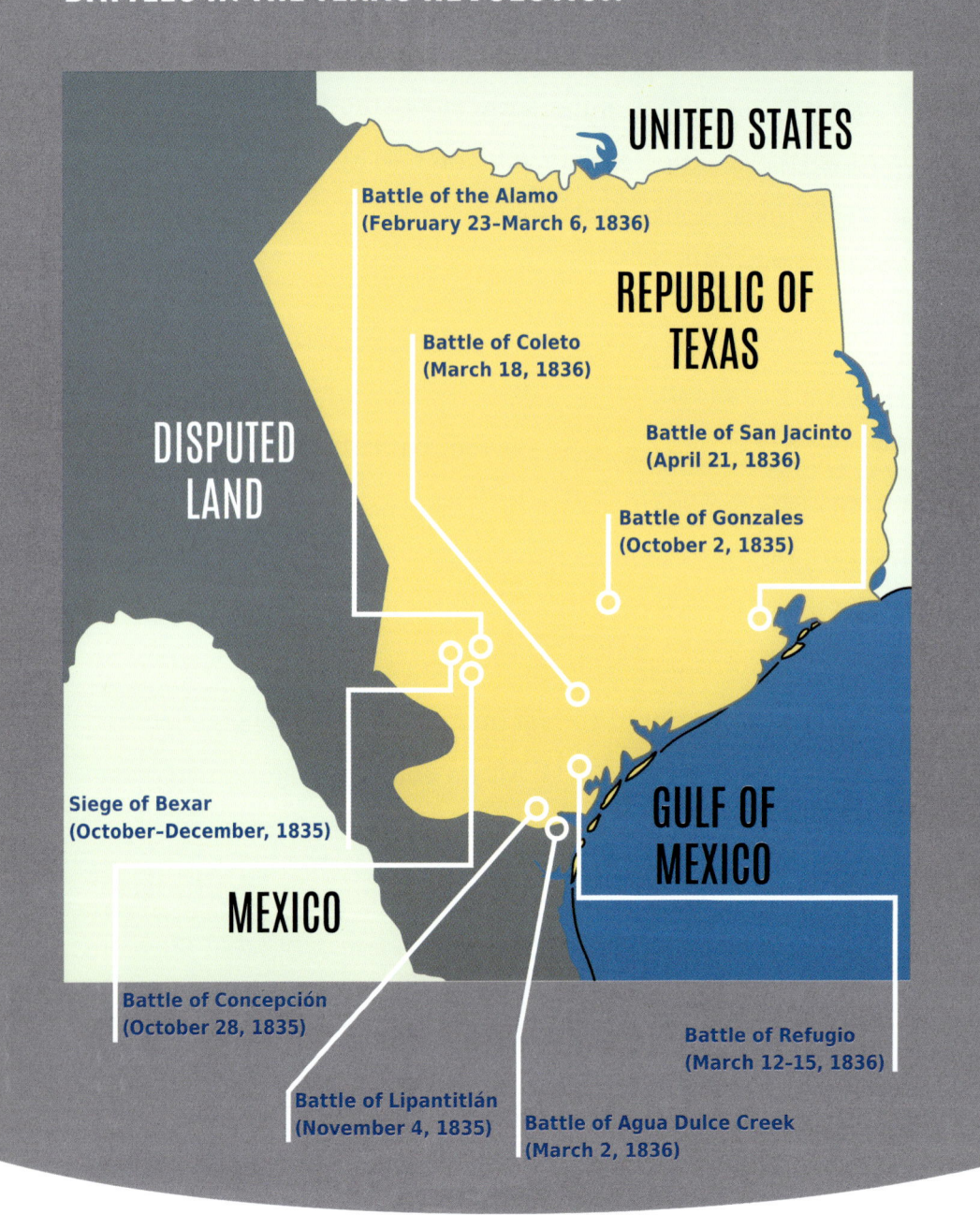

**UNITED STATES**

Battle of the Alamo
(February 23–March 6, 1836)

**REPUBLIC OF TEXAS**

Battle of Coleto
(March 18, 1836)

Battle of San Jacinto
(April 21, 1836)

**DISPUTED LAND**

Battle of Gonzales
(October 2, 1835)

Siege of Bexar
(October–December, 1835)

**GULF OF MEXICO**

**MEXICO**

Battle of Concepción
(October 28, 1835)

Battle of Refugio
(March 12–15, 1836)

Battle of Lipantitlán
(November 4, 1835)

Battle of Agua Dulce Creek
(March 2, 1836)

Before the sun rose, a group crept quietly down Acequia Street in San Antonio. Another group went down Soledad Street. A third group crossed the river with a cannon and moved toward the Alamo. The Alamo was an old Spanish mission. Missions were used by Europeans to try to force Native Americans to believe in Christianity.

When everyone was in position, the cannon would fire. That would be the signal to begin the attack. All the troops arrived in their designated spots. They waited in the darkness. The only sound they heard was the wind and an occasional **sentry** doing rounds. At 5:00 a.m., the sound of a cannon being fired cracked through the air. The Mexican troops were quick to respond. Soldiers from both sides ran toward each other and shouted. Gunfire roared.

The Texans advanced on San Antonio's city plaza. Cannons were stationed there, and the Mexican soldiers fired them through slits in the plaza's **palisades**. The Texans moved forward and broke into nearby buildings for shelter.

But as the days went on, the Texans were in a difficult position. One man had died and 15 more were wounded. They were tired, and their cannon no longer worked. The Mexicans still had working cannons and fired them frequently. The Mexicans also had three times as many soldiers as the Texans.

▲ The Texans' invasion of San Antonio sparked the Battle of the Alamo.

But Milam's group moved forward through the city and captured houses along the way. They slowly made progress.

The sun was high in the sky on December 7 as Milam looked over the battlefield with field glasses, which were like binoculars, to survey the damage. Light on the glasses caused a reflection.

A Mexican **sniper** sitting in a tree saw the reflection and fired. Milam died instantly.

The Texans were upset to have lost their leader, but they kept fighting. As the battle went on, the Mexicans lost more ground.

▲ David Crockett, a former U.S. politician, arrived in San Antonio after the Texans' victory. He fought in the Battle of the Alamo.

The Mexican leader, General Martín Perfecto de Cos, came up with a new plan. He decided to attack the Texans' camp near San Antonio. Cos knew that if he could capture their camp, the Texans would have to leave San Antonio to defend it. Part of the Mexican force marched out of San Antonio to the Texans' camp. But Burleson was one step ahead of Cos. He had soldiers and guns at the camp. Cos's men were met with cannon fire as they approached. The Mexicans had to retreat.

Late on December 8 in San Antonio, the Texans had taken over all but one major building, which the Mexicans held. The Texans charged. They used crowbars, rifles, and knives to get into the building. The Mexicans could not withstand the attack. The next day, Cos admitted that the Mexicans had lost. A peace **treaty** was arranged, and Cos led his men away from San Antonio.

Mexican President Antonio López de Santa Anna was angry when he heard of his army's defeat. When Cos and his men arrived home, Santa Anna made it clear to them that the fight against the Texans was not over. He ordered his army to rest, regroup, and fight again. Santa Anna was sure they would win next time.

James Bowie was one of the soldiers at the Alamo. A statue of him is in Texarkana, Texas. ▶

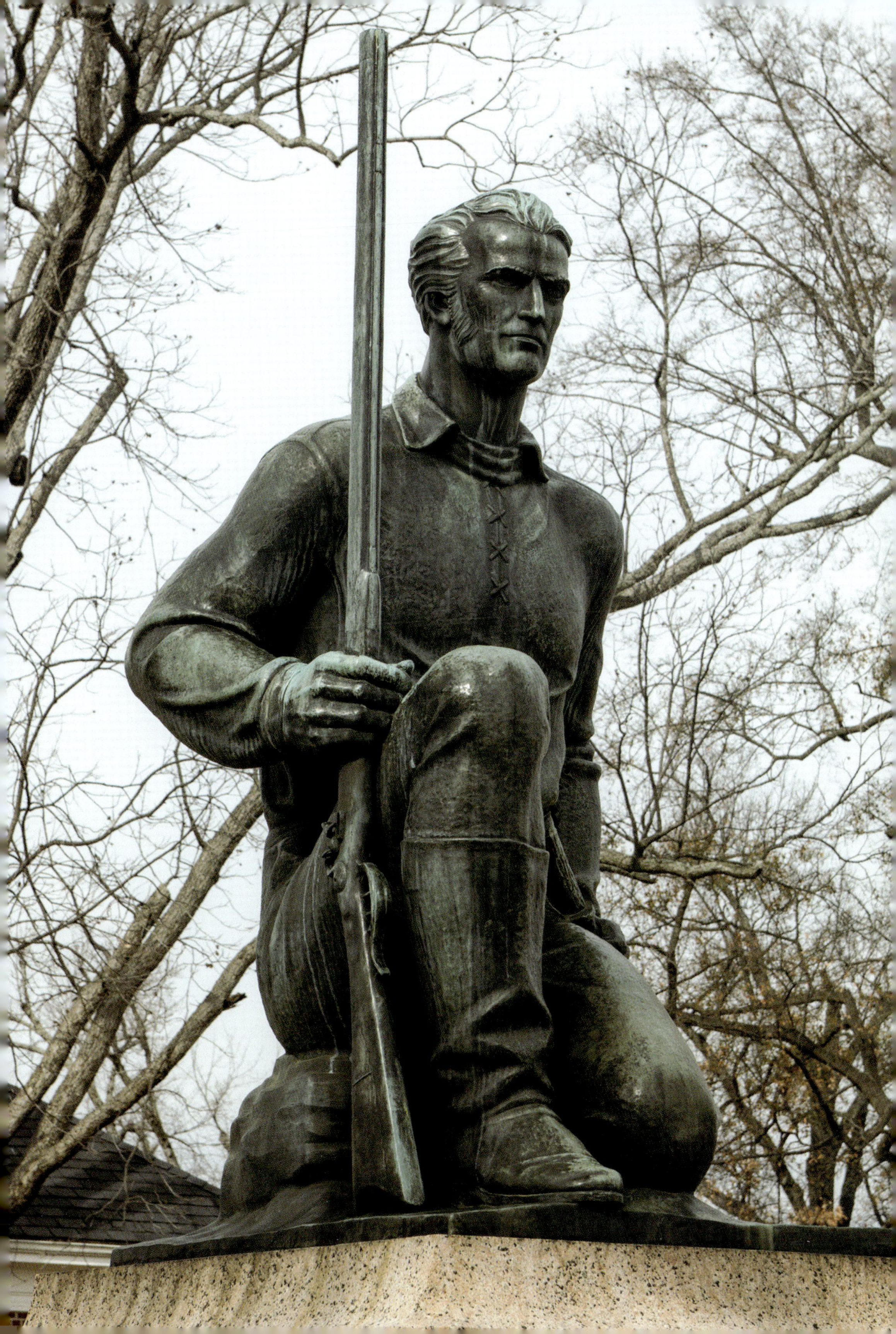

Chapter 2

# THE BATTLE OF THE ALAMO

As the sun brushed the horizon on March 5, 1836, things looked grim for the Texans. They had taken shelter at the Alamo and had begun turning it into a battle fort. It was the only fort standing between the Mexican soldiers and nearby Texan settlements.

◀ **Texan fighters didn't stand a chance against the Mexican forces at the Alamo.**

The Texan soldiers knew it was important to keep the Alamo out of Mexico's control. This would prevent the Mexicans from taking over the settlements. Looking out from the Alamo that morning, the Texans could see more than 1,000 Mexican soldiers. The Alamo had been under siege since February 23. The Texans watched the large Mexican force nervously. The Mexicans had enough soldiers to overpower them. The Texans had fewer than 300 men. Santa Anna was leading the Mexicans. He gave the Texans the chance to surrender.

William Travis, a lieutenant colonel, was leading the Alamo forces. He felt strongly that Texas should be part of the United States. Even though the Mexicans outnumbered them, he did not want to surrender. But the Texans were trapped in the Alamo and did not have enough supplies for a long siege. Travis sent letters to surrounding settlements and to the United States, asking for money and troops. The lack of response from his letters frustrated him. He wrote to a friend, "If my countrymen do not rally to my relief, I am determined to perish in the defense of this place, and my bones shall reproach my country for her neglect."[2]

It seemed clear to everyone that the Alamo would fall. All the Mexicans had to do was wait for the Texans to use up their food.

▲ Antonio López de Santa Anna ordered his troops to attack the Alamo from four directions.

Then the Texans would have to surrender. But Santa Anna was impatient. On March 5, he decided to attack the Alamo. His men pointed out that the Texans would have to surrender eventually.

The Mexican men didn't agree with his decision. They asked Santa Anna why he would risk Mexican lives. But Santa Anna did not listen. Mexican Captain José Sanchez was upset with him.

▲ The Texans at the Alamo were determined to fight for Texas's independence.

He wrote, "Why is it that Señor Santa Anna always wants his triumphs and defeats to be marked by blood and tears?"[3]

Early the next day before the sun had risen, Texan Captain John Baugh walked around the Alamo. It was very quiet. Baugh checked each defender's spot in the fort. There were multiple firearms laid out. Some of the guns had sharp **bayonets**.

At 5:30 a.m., Mexican bugler José Gonzalez sounded the opening battle cry. The sound of the bugle, which is an instrument like a small trumpet, echoed through the silent morning air. Baugh's heart leaped when he heard it. He ran to Travis's quarters and yelled, "Colonel Travis, the Mexicans are coming!"[4]

The Texans sped to their posts. They watched as the Mexicans put up ladders outside the Alamo walls. Travis grabbed a rifle and bent over the wall to shoot at the Mexicans. But as he aimed, he was shot and killed instantly.

By 6:30 a.m. the battle was over. All of the Texas fighting men had died, either in the battle or when they were captured. The Mexicans had won a sweeping victory. It seemed unlikely that Texas would ever have the strength to beat the Mexican Army and win its independence.

San Antonio, Texas, has a monument honoring the ▶ Texan soldiers.

TRAVIS                    CROCKETT

## Chapter 3

# THE BATTLE ENDS

Susannah Dickinson was in the Alamo during the battle. Her husband was one of the soldiers trying to defend it. As the Alamo was attacked, she grabbed her baby daughter, Angelina. She clutched the child to her body and ran to the Alamo's church with other women and children. They huddled together. They did not know if the church building would protect them, but it felt like their only hope.

◀ Today the Alamo is a historic landmark.

Dickinson heard shouts and cries outside. Cannons fired. The church building itself felt like it was under attack. She had no way of knowing how the battle was going. Her daughter began wailing. Then, a Mexican officer came to the door and asked for Dickinson. At first, she was too frightened to answer. Then he said, "If you want to save your life, follow me."[5]

He led Dickinson and her daughter out of the church. Once outside, she heard a loud gunshot nearby. Dickinson's right shin was hit by the bullet, and she cried out in pain. The officer helped her and her daughter into a buggy, which took them to a friend's house in San Antonio. Earlier, the friend had visited Santa Anna and begged him to spare Dickinson's life.

Santa Anna sent Dickinson and her daughter to the Texas camp at Gonzalez. They were to deliver a letter of warning to Sam Houston. The letter said that if Houston did not retreat, he and his men would meet the same fate as the men at the Alamo. Santa Anna meant what he wrote. He pushed his army farther into Texas. He was determined to beat the Texans at any cost. Terrified Texan settlers scrambled to leave the area.

The **massacre** at the Alamo attracted attention. Houston began gathering troops to fight back. On April 21, 1836, a new batch of Texan troops battled a Mexican force at San Jacinto.

▲ Santa Anna fought for Mexico's independence from Spain in 1821.

San Jacinto is in present-day Texas. The Texans had approximately 900 men, and they faced a Mexican force of 1,300 men. But the Texans attacked the Mexicans in a surprise raid. As the Texans attacked, they shouted, "Remember the Alamo!"[6] The battle lasted 18 minutes, and this time the Texans won.

Sam Houston was wounded in the Battle of San Jacinto. ▶

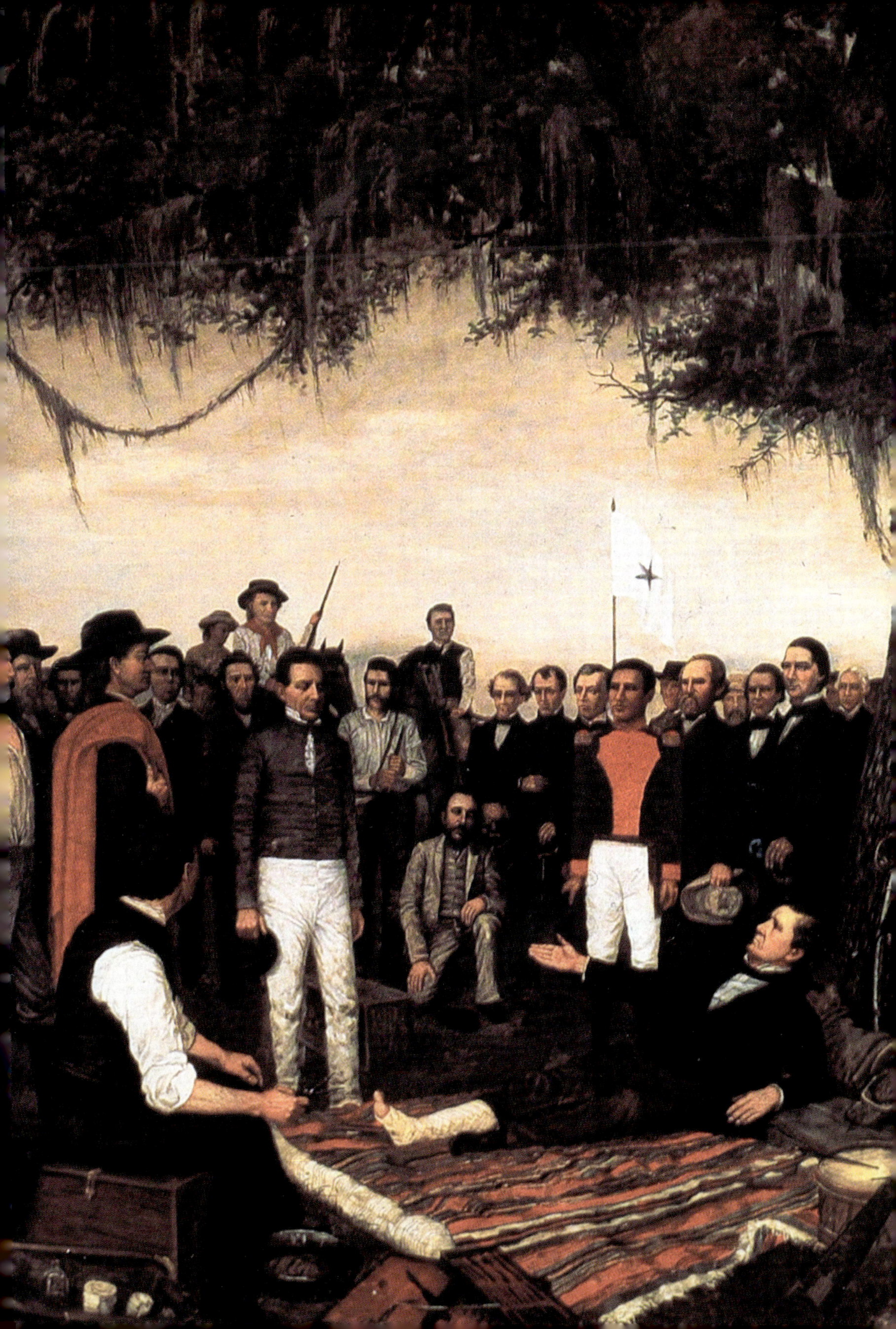

## Chapter 4

# AFTER THE ALAMO

Houston smiled as he was named the first president of the Republic of Texas on September 5, 1836. The war had been won. Texas was now free from Mexico's rule. A crowd of cheering supporters welcomed him into his new role.

However, Mexico still considered Texas to be part of a Mexican state, even though other nations recognized Texas as an independent country.

◀ San Fernando Cathedral in San Antonio claims to have the remains of the Alamo heroes. But many historians don't think the remains are from Alamo soldiers.

Houston wanted the United States to **annex** Texas and make it one of the country's states. Many people agreed. But Houston knew that the U.S. government was hesitant to do this. The U.S. government was worried that Mexico would start a war if the United States annexed Texas. Also, Texas was a slave-holding region. Many people in the U.S. government were opposed to adding another slave-holding state to the nation.

Years later, in 1843, Great Britain's leaders were worried. They did not want the United States to expand and become more powerful. So they told the United States that they opposed Texas's annexation.

President John Tyler paced around his home when he heard the news. He was afraid Great Britain would try to make Texas an **ally** against the United States. He began working to convince members of Congress to annex Texas. By 1845, Tyler and then-president James Polk convinced Congress to agree to the annexation. Texas became a state on December 29, 1845.

However, that was not the end of the conflict with Mexico. Polk wanted to get ahold of more land that was held by Mexico. That land includes areas of California and New Mexico today.

▲ James Polk took office in 1845. He was the 11th U.S. president.

On April 25, 1846, war broke out along the Rio Grande and continued moving west over several months. The first battles went badly for Mexico. The U.S. forces outfought the Mexicans.

By late 1847, it was clear that the United States would win. In February 1848, the Treaty of Guadeloupe was signed. It named the Rio Grande as the southern border of the United States.

▲ Anson Jones was the last president of the Republic of Texas. When Texas became a state, Jones removed the Texas flag from the capitol building.

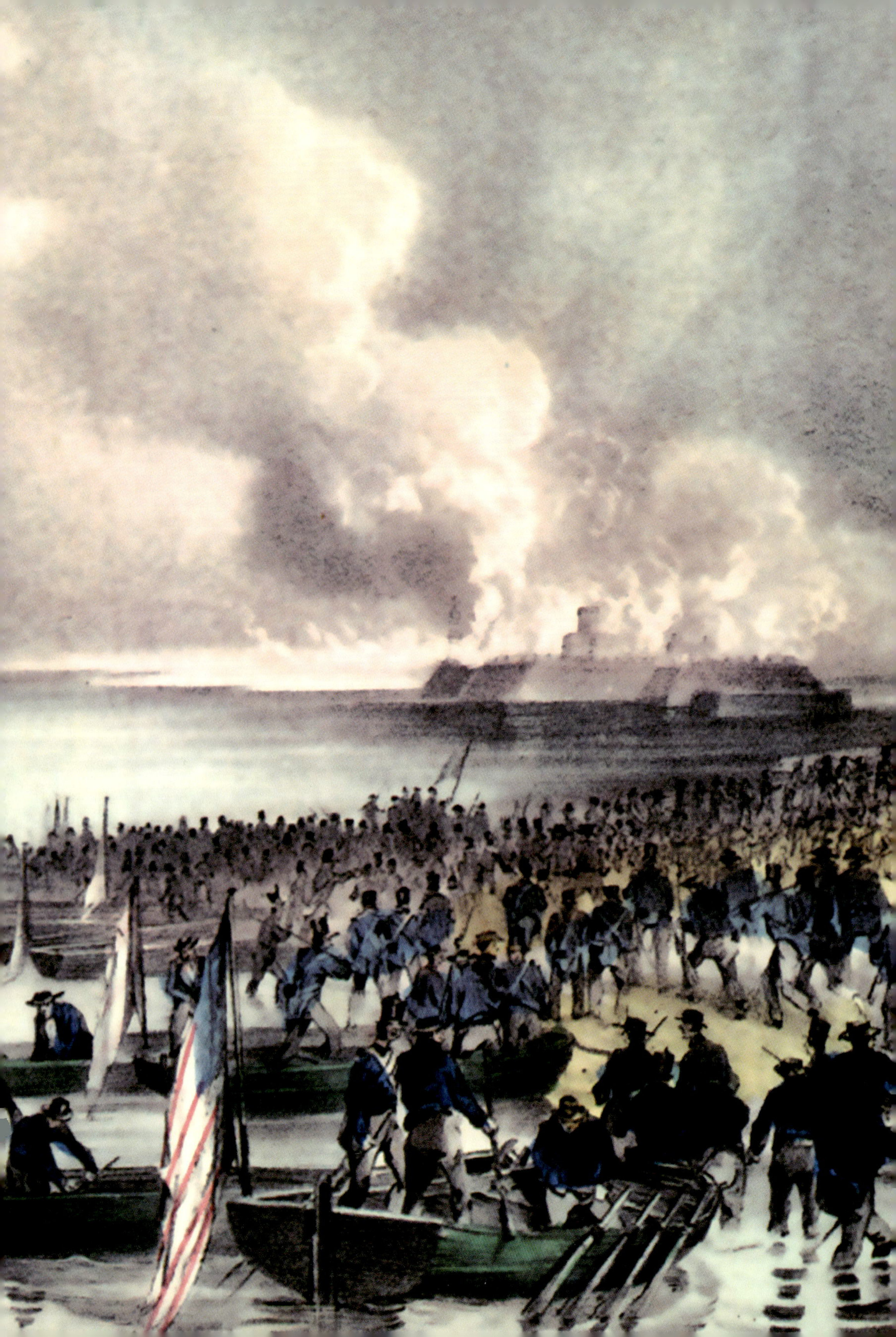

It forced Mexico to recognize Texas as part of the United States. It also allowed the United States to buy California and the land northwest of the Rio Grande from Mexico. The southern border of the United States was final. Although they weren't there to see it, the men who fought at the Alamo succeeded in their fight for independence from Mexico.

## THINK ABOUT IT

- Why was it important for the U.S. settlers in Texas to fight for independence from Mexico?
- Why do you think the Texans at the Alamo were willing to fight against the much larger Mexican forces?
- After the massacre at the Alamo, many men shouted "Remember the Alamo!" as they rode into battle at San Jacinto. Why did they say this? What did it mean to the soldiers?

◀ U.S. troops captured Veracruz, a Mexican port, during the war.

# GLOSSARY

**ally (AL-eye):** An ally is a country that is on the same side as another country during a conflict. John Tyler didn't want Texas to become an ally of Great Britain.

**annex (uh-NEKS):** To annex is to take control of or join together. The United States wanted to annex Texas.

**bayonets (BAY-uh-nets):** Bayonets are steel blades attached to the end of long rifles. Some Texas soldiers had bayonets on their guns.

**massacre (MASS-uh-kur):** A massacre is the destruction of a large number of people. Sam Houston gathered troops to fight back after the Alamo massacre.

**palisades (pal-uh-SAYDZ):** Palisades are a series of tall, strong, pointed stakes set at the top of walls for defense. Mexican soldiers fired cannons from palisades.

**republic (ri-PUHB-lik):** A republic is a government that is led by an elected official. Sam Houston was the president of the Republic of Texas.

**sentry (SEN-tree):** A sentry is a soldier who stands guard. Texan soldiers hid from a sentry in San Antonio.

**siege (SEEJ):** A siege is when an army surrounds a place in order to force the people inside to surrender. The Alamo underwent a siege by the Mexican forces.

**sniper (SNIPE-er):** A sniper is a shooter who hides as he or she shoots. A sniper killed Ben Milam.

**treaty (TREE-tee):** A treaty is an agreement drawn up between political groups. The United States and Mexico signed a treaty.

# SOURCE NOTES

1. Edwin P. Hoyt. *The Alamo: An Illustrated History*. Dallas, TX: Taylor Publishing, 1999. Print. 56.

2. "Alamo, Battle of the." *Texas State Historical Association*. Texas State Historical Association, n.d. Web. 21 Dec. 2017.

3. Edwin P. Hoyt. *The Alamo: An Illustrated History*. Dallas, TX: Taylor Publishing, 1999. Print. 67–69.

4. Jim Donovan. *The Blood of Heroes*. New York, NY: Little, Brown and Co., 2012. Print. 277.

5. Edwin P. Hoyt. *The Alamo: An Illustrated History*. Dallas, TX: Taylor Publishing, 1999. Print. 121.

6. "Texas Revolution." *Texas State Historical Association*. Texas State Historical Association, n.d. Web. 21 Dec. 2017.

# TO LEARN MORE

## Books

Collins, Phil. *The Alamo and Beyond: A Collector's Journey*. Buffalo Gap, TX: State House Press, 2012.

Harasymiw, Therese. *Causes and Effects of the Texas Revolution*. New York, NY: Rosen, 2010.

Pollack, Pam and Meg Belviso. *What Was the Alamo?* New York, NY: Grosset & Dunlap, 2013.

## Web Sites

Visit our Web site for links about the Battle of the Alamo: childsworld.com/links

*Note to Parents, Teachers, and Librarians: We routinely verify our Web links to make sure they are safe and active sites. So encourage your readers to check them out!*

# INDEX

Alamo, 5, 9, 14, 15, 16, 18, 20, 21, 22, 29

battle fort, 14, 18

Baugh, John, 18

Burleson, Edward, 6, 7, 12

cannons, 9, 12, 21

Dickinson, Susannah, 20, 21

Houston, Sam, 5, 7, 21, 24, 25

independence, 7, 18, 24, 29

Milam, Ben, 6, 7, 10, 11

Republic of Texas, 7, 8, 24, 25

Rio Grande, 26, 27, 29

San Antonio, 5, 6, 7, 9, 12, 21

San Jacinto, 5, 21, 22

Sanchez, José, 17, 18

Santa Anna, Antonio López de, 4, 5, 12, 15, 16, 17, 18, 21

sentry, 9

settlements, 14, 15

settlers, 4, 21

siege, 5, 7, 8, 15

supplies, 15

surrender, 15, 16

Travis, William, 15, 18

treaty, 12, 27

32